AI Language Models: Your New Secret Weapon

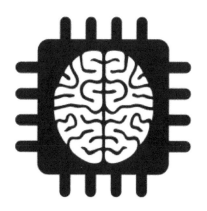

P.A Hopper

AI Language Models: Your New Secret Weapon

AI Language Models: Your New Secret Weapon is a comprehensive guide to understanding and utilizing AI language models to enhance communication and productivity. This book covers the basics of natural language processing, advanced techniques for improving language models, use cases for AI language models, and best practices for implementation. It also includes case studies of successful implementation and a step-by-step guide for building your own language model. The future of AI language models is also explored, with insights into the latest advancements and potential applications in various industries. Written in an engaging and accessible style, this book is perfect for anyone looking to stay ahead of the curve and leverage the power of AI language models in their business or personal projects. Whether you're a beginner or an experienced developer, AI Language Models: Your New Secret Weapon is an essential resource for anyone interested in the world of AI language models.

CONTENTS

Chapter 00 Introduction
Red Pill Blue Pill

Artificial intelligence (AI) language models are rapidly transforming the way we communicate, work, and interact with technology. These models, which are powered by sophisticated algorithms and machine learning techniques, are capable of analyzing vast amounts of text data and generating human-like responses to natural language queries. As a result, they are becoming an increasingly important tool for businesses, organizations, and individuals looking to streamline their operations, improve customer experiences, and gain a competitive edge.

In this book, we'll explore the world of AI language models and show you how to make them your new secret weapon. We'll start by providing an overview of what AI language models are and how they work, and we'll cover some of the key concepts and terminology associated with this technology. From there, we'll dive into the practicalities of using AI language models, including how to get started, how to choose the right model, and how to train your own model.

We'll also explore some of the most common use cases for AI language models, such as customer service, marketing, and healthcare, and we'll showcase some real-world examples of how businesses and organizations are using this technology to achieve their goals. Along the way, we'll discuss some of the ethical considerations associated with AI language models, and we'll explore emerging trends and technologies that are shaping the future of this field.

Whether you're a student, a professional, or simply someone interested in learning more about the exciting world of AI language models, this book will provide you with the insights, knowledge, and practical guidance you need to get started. So, let's dive in and discover the power of AI language models together!

Chapter 5 will provide you with best practices for using AI language models, including how to optimize performance, how to handle bias and fairness concerns, and how to integrate with other technologies. We'll also explore some of the common challenges and pitfalls associated with using AI language models, and provide tips and tricks for avoiding them.

In Chapter 6, we'll look to the future and explore emerging trends and technologies that are shaping the future of AI language models. We'll discuss advances in conversational AI, machine learning, and deep learning, and explore some of the ways in which AI language models are likely to evolve and become even more powerful and versatile in the years to come.

Finally, in Chapter 7, we'll provide case studies of real-world examples of how organizations and individuals are using AI language models to achieve their goals. These case studies will showcase the wide range of applications and use cases for AI language models, and demonstrate the power and versatility of this technology.

By the end of this book, you'll have a deep understanding of what AI language models are, how they work, and how they can be used to achieve a wide range of business and personal objectives. You'll also have the practical skills and knowledge needed to get started with using AI language models in your own projects and applications.

So, whether you're a business owner, a marketer, a data scientist, or simply someone curious about the potential of AI language models, this book is for you. Let's get started!

Chapter 01 Rabbit Hole
Getting Started with AI Language Models

1.1 What Are AI Language Models?

Definition and overview of AI language models Types of AI language models (rule-based, statistical, and neural network-based models) Examples of AI language models in action

1.2 How Do AI Language Models Work?

Introduction to natural language processing (NLP) The role of machine learning in NLP and AI language models Overview of the training process and how AI language models learn from data

1.3 Key Concepts and Terminology

Understanding text corpus, tokens, embeddings, and language models Explaining key concepts such as input/output, context, and semantic meaning.

1.4 Popular AI Language Models

Overview of popular AI language models such as GPT-3, BERT, and ELMo Comparison of different AI language models and their use cases Advantages and limitations of different models

1.5 Setting Up Your Environment

Overview of tools and resources needed to work with AI language models Examples of programming languages, libraries, and frameworks used in AI language models Steps to set up your environment for building and training AI language models.

1.6 Choosing the Right AI Language Model

Factors to consider when choosing an AI language model for your use case Understanding the trade-offs between accuracy, speed, and cost Best practices for selecting and evaluating AI language models.

1.1 What Are AI Language Models?

AI language models are a type of artificial intelligence that uses natural language processing (NLP) to generate text. They are designed to analyze and understand human language and produce natural-sounding responses to questions, prompts, or commands. There are three types of AI language models: rule-based, statistical, and neural network-based models. Rule-based models use pre-defined rules to generate responses, while statistical models rely on probability distributions and machine learning algorithms to generate text. Neural network-based models use deep learning techniques to analyze vast amounts of data and generate text that is more human-like than traditional statistical models.

Examples of AI language models include virtual assistants like Siri and Alexa, chatbots for customer service, and language translation tools like Google Translate.

1.2 How Do AI Language Models Work?

AI language models work by analyzing large amounts of text data to learn patterns in language usage, such as sentence structure, vocabulary, and grammar. They use these patterns to generate new text that sounds like it was written by a human. The process of training an AI language model involves feeding it large amounts of text data, such as books, articles, or social media posts. The model then analyzes the data to learn patterns in language usage and builds a probabilistic model that can predict the likelihood of certain words or phrases appearing in a given context.

When a user inputs text into an AI language model, the model uses its learned knowledge to generate a response. For example, if a user asks a chatbot a question, the model will analyze the question and generate a response based on its learned knowledge of language usage.

1.3 Key Concepts and Terminology

To understand AI language models, it's important to be familiar with key concepts and terminology associated with this technology. Some of these concepts include:

Text corpus: a large collection of text data used to train an AI language model.

Tokens: individual words or phrases that make up a sentence or piece of text. **Embeddings:** a numerical representation of words or phrases that allows AI language models to analyze and understand language.

Language models: a statistical model that predicts the probability of a given sequence of words. Input/output: the process of feeding input data into an AI language model and receiving an output response.

Context: the surrounding words or phrases that provide meaning to a particular word or phrase.

Semantic meaning: the meaning behind a particular word or phrase, taking into account the context in which it is used.

1.4 Popular AI Language Models

There are several popular AI language models in use today, including:

GPT-3 (Generative Pre-trained Transformer 3): a neural network-based language model that uses deep learning to generate human-like text.

BERT (Bidirectional Encoder Representations from Transformers): a neural network-based model that is designed to understand the context of a given word or phrase and generate responses that are more relevant and accurate.

ELMo (Embeddings from Language Models): a neural network-based model that uses contextualized embeddings to generate more accurate and relevant responses.

Each of these models has its own strengths and weaknesses, and the choice of which one to use depends on the specific use case.

1.5 Setting Up Your Environment

To work with AI language models, you'll need access to the right tools and resources. Some common programming languages used in AI language models include Python, R, and Java. You'll also need access to libraries and frameworks such as TensorFlow, PyTorch, and Keras. Setting up your environment for building and training AI language models can be complex, but there are several resources available to help you get started. Some popular resources include online tutorials, open source projects, and cloud-based services that offer pre-configured environments for building and training AI language models.

Cloud-based services like Google Cloud Platform, Microsoft Azure, and Amazon Web Services offer pre-configured environments and tools for building and training AI language models. These services also provide access to large amounts of data and computing resources, making it easier to train complex models. In addition to cloud-based services, there are also open-source libraries and frameworks that can help you build and train AI language models. Some popular libraries include NLTK (Natural Language Toolkit), SpaCy, and Gensim. Frameworks like TensorFlow and PyTorch also offer tools and resources for building and training AI language models.

It's important to choose the right tools and resources for your specific use case, as well as to ensure that you have the necessary computing resources to train complex models.

1.6 Conclusion

AI language models have revolutionized the way we interact with computers and have opened up new possibilities for natural language processing and generation. In this chapter, we've introduced the key concepts and terminology associated with AI language models and discussed some of the popular models in use today. We've also talked about the importance of setting up your environment with the right tools and resources to build and train AI language models. In the next chapter, we'll explore how to use AI language models in practical applications.

Chapter 02 NLP
Natural Language Processing

Natural Language Processing (NLP) is a subfield of artificial intelligence that deals with the interaction between computers and human languages. It involves tasks such as text processing, text analysis, and text generation, all of which require an understanding of the structure and meaning of human language.

In this chapter, we'll cover some of the basic concepts of NLP, including tokenization, part-of-speech tagging, and named entity recognition.

2.2 Tokenization

Tokenization is the process of breaking up a piece of text into smaller units, called tokens. These tokens could be words, punctuation marks, or even individual characters. Tokenization is an important step in many NLP tasks, as it provides a way to standardize the input text and make it easier to process.

For example, consider the sentence "The quick brown fox jumps over the lazy dog." Tokenization of this sentence might result in the following tokens:

The

quick

brown

fox

jumps

over

the

lazy

dog

.

2.3 Part-of-Speech Tagging

Part-of-speech (POS) tagging is the process of labeling each word in a piece of text with its corresponding part of speech, such as noun, verb, or adjective. POS tagging is important for many NLP tasks, including text classification, sentiment analysis, and named entity recognition.

For example, consider the sentence "I ate a delicious sandwich for lunch." A POS tagger might label the words as follows:

I (pronoun)

ate (verb)

a (determiner)

delicious (adjective)

sandwich (noun)

for (preposition)

lunch (noun)

. (punctuation)

2.4 Named Entity Recognition

Named Entity Recognition (NER) is the process of identifying and classifying named entities in a piece of text, such as people, organizations, and locations. NER is important for many NLP tasks, including information extraction and question answering.

For example, consider the sentence "Barack Obama was born in Hawaii and served as President of the United States." NER might identify "Barack Obama" as a person, "Hawaii" as a location, and "President of the United States" as a job title.

In this chapter, we've covered some of the basic concepts of NLP, including tokenization, part-of-speech tagging, and named entity recognition. These concepts are fundamental to many NLP tasks, and understanding them is important for building and using AI language models. In the next chapter, we'll explore some practical applications of AI language models in various industries.

2.5 Practical Applications of AI Language Models

AI language models have a wide range of practical applications in various industries, including healthcare, finance, and marketing. In this section, we'll explore some examples of how AI language models are being used in these industries.

2.6 Healthcare

AI language models are being used in healthcare to improve patient outcomes and streamline operations. One example is the use of AI language models for medical coding, which involves translating medical terms and diagnoses into standardized codes for billing and insurance purposes. AI language models can help automate this process, reducing the time and errors associated with manual coding.

Another example is the use of AI language models for clinical decision support, which involves using AI to help healthcare providers make more informed treatment decisions. AI language models can analyze patient data and medical literature to provide personalized treatment recommendations and identify potential risks.

2.7 Finance

AI language models are also being used in finance to improve risk management and fraud detection. For example, AI language models can analyze text data from financial reports and news articles to identify potential risks and trends in the market. Another example is the use of AI language models for fraud detection, which involves analyzing text data from financial transactions to identify suspicious activity. AI language models can help flag potential fraud cases and reduce false positives, saving financial institutions time and money.

2.8 Marketing

AI language models are being used in marketing to improve customer engagement and personalization. For example, AI language models can analyze customer feedback and social media data to identify sentiment and preferences, helping companies tailor their marketing strategies to specific customer segments. Another example is the use of AI language models for chatbots and virtual assistants, which can provide personalized customer support and recommendations. AI language models can understand natural language queries and provide relevant responses, improving the customer experience and reducing the workload for customer support teams.

2.8 Conclusion

AI language models have a wide range of practical applications in various industries, including healthcare, finance, and marketing. By leveraging the power of natural language processing and generation, these models can help automate tasks, improve decision-making, and provide personalized experiences for customers.

Chapter 03 Advanced NLP techniques
Improve AI language models

In this chapter, we'll explore some advanced NLP techniques that can be used to improve AI language models. These techniques include:

3.1 Transfer Learning

Transfer learning is a technique that involves pre-training a language model on a large corpus of text data and then fine-tuning it on a smaller, domain-specific dataset. This approach can help improve the performance of the language model on the target task, as it has already learned useful representations of language from the pre-training data. *For example, a language model pre-trained on a large corpus of news articles could be fine-tuned on a smaller dataset of financial reports to improve its performance on financial text data.*

3.2 Named Entity Recognition

Named entity recognition (NER) is a technique that involves identifying and categorizing named entities in text data, such as people, organizations, and locations. This technique can be used to improve the accuracy of language models by providing additional context and information about the text. *For example, a language model trained on news articles could be improved by incorporating NER to identify the names of people, organizations, and locations mentioned in the articles.*

3.3 Sentiment Analysis

Sentiment analysis is a technique that involves identifying the sentiment or emotion expressed in text data, such as positive, negative, or neutral. This technique can be used to improve the accuracy of language models by providing additional context and information about the text. *For example, a language model trained on customer reviews could be improved by incorporating sentiment analysis to identify the overall sentiment expressed in each review.*

3.4 Text Summarization

Text summarization is a technique that involves generating a summary of a longer text, such as an article or document. This technique can be used to improve the efficiency and accuracy of language models by reducing the amount of text data they need to process. *For example, a language model used for news article analysis could be improved by incorporating text summarization to generate a summary of each article, allowing the model to process more articles in less time.*

3.5 Language Generation

Language generation is a technique that involves generating new text data based on a given input, such as a prompt or topic. This technique can be used to improve the creativity and versatility of language models by allowing them to generate new text that is not present in the training data. *For example, a language model trained on a corpus of literature could be used to generate new stories or poems based on a given prompt or theme.*

3.6 Conclusion

By incorporating these advanced NLP techniques, AI language models can be improved in a variety of ways, including increased accuracy, efficiency, and creativity. In the next chapter, we'll explore some best practices for training and fine-tuning AI language models.

Chapter 04 Use Gold
Use Cases for AI Language Models

In this chapter, we'll explore some of the most common use cases for AI language models. These use cases include:

5.1 Text Classification

Text classification is a task that involves assigning a label or category to a piece of text, such as determining whether an email is spam or not. AI language models can be trained to perform text classification tasks, allowing businesses to automate processes such as customer support or email filtering.

5.2 Chatbots

Chatbots are computer programs that use natural language processing to interact with users in a conversational manner. AI language models can be used to power chatbots, allowing businesses to provide 24/7 customer support without the need for human operators.

5.3 Sentiment Analysis

As mentioned earlier, sentiment analysis is a technique that involves identifying the sentiment expressed in a piece of text. AI language models can be used for sentiment analysis in a variety of applications, such as social media monitoring or market research.

5.4 Machine Translation

Machine translation is the task of automatically translating text from one language to another. AI language models can be used for machine translation, allowing businesses to expand their global reach and communicate with customers in different languages.

5.5 Text Generation

Text generation is the task of automatically generating text based on a given prompt or theme. AI language models can be used for text generation in a variety of applications, such as content creation or storytelling.

5.6 Conclusion

AI language models have a wide range of use cases, from automating customer support to expanding a business's global reach. By understanding these use cases, businesses can identify opportunities to incorporate AI language models into their operations and gain a competitive edge. In the next chapter, we'll explore some of the ethical considerations surrounding the use of AI language models.

Chapter 05
Ethical Considerations for AI Language Models

AI language models have the potential to transform the way we interact with technology, but with that potential comes a range of ethical considerations that businesses and individuals need to consider.

6.1 Bias

One of the primary ethical concerns with AI language models is the issue of bias. Bias can arise when the data used to train these models is not representative of the population it is intended to serve. For example, a model trained solely on data from white males may not accurately represent the experiences of women or people of color. This can lead to inaccurate results or perpetuate existing biases.

To address this issue, businesses need to be proactive in ensuring that the data used to train their AI language models is diverse and representative of the population it is intended to serve. This can involve collecting data from a range of sources and using techniques such as oversampling to ensure that all groups are represented.

6.2 Privacy

AI language models often rely on large amounts of personal data to function effectively. This can include everything from email and text messages to social media posts and online search history. As such, businesses have a responsibility to be transparent with their customers about how their data is being used and to ensure that it is being used in a responsible and ethical manner.

To address this issue, businesses should consider implementing policies and practices that prioritize data privacy and security. This can involve implementing robust data protection protocols, such as data encryption and access controls, and being transparent about how customer data is being used.

6.3 Accountability

AI language models can make mistakes, just like humans. However, it can be difficult to determine who is responsible when something goes wrong. As such, businesses need to take steps to ensure that they are accountable for the actions of their AI language models. To address this issue, businesses should consider implementing clear lines of accountability for their AI language models. This can involve appointing a dedicated team to oversee the development and deployment of these models, implementing rigorous testing and validation protocols, and being transparent with customers about how these models are being used.

6.4 Conclusion

As AI language models become more ubiquitous, it is increasingly important for businesses and individuals to consider the ethical implications of their use. By addressing issues such as bias, privacy, and accountability, businesses can ensure that they are using these models in a responsible and ethical manner, while also unlocking their potential to transform the way we communicate and interact with technology. In the final chapter, we'll explore some tips for getting started with AI language models.

Chapter 06
Best Practices for Using AI Language Models

AI language models have the potential to revolutionize the way we communicate and interact with technology. However, to realize the full potential of these models, it is essential to adopt best practices for their development, deployment, and maintenance.

7.1 Data Preparation

The quality of the data used to train AI language models is critical to their accuracy and effectiveness. As such, it is essential to prioritize data preparation as part of the development process. This can involve tasks such as data cleaning, normalization, and preprocessing. *For example, consider the development of a chatbot for customer service. To ensure that the chatbot is effective, it is essential to train it on a diverse set of customer inquiries and responses. This may involve collecting and preprocessing customer support data from a* range of sources, such as email, social media, and phone conversations, to create a comprehensive training dataset.

7.2 Model Selection and Tuning

The selection of the appropriate AI language model is critical to the success of any project. Different models may perform better on different tasks, depending on factors such as data volume and complexity. It is also important to consider the tradeoff between model complexity and accuracy.

Once a model has been selected, it is essential to tune it to the specific use case. This can involve fine-tuning the model parameters or adjusting the training data to optimize performance. *For example, consider the development of a sentiment analysis model for product reviews. The choice of the appropriate model architecture and the selection of relevant features such as word embeddings, can have a significant impact on model performance. Tuning hyperparameters such as learning rate and batch size can further optimize model accuracy.*

7.3 Testing and Validation

Testing and validation are essential components of the development process for AI language models. These processes help to identify and correct errors or inconsistencies in the model's performance before it is deployed. To test the effectiveness of an AI language model, it is essential to use a range of evaluation metrics such as accuracy, precision, and recall. The use of a test dataset that is independent of the training data can help to identify potential bias or overfitting issues. *For example, consider the development of a machine translation model for medical documents. Testing the model's accuracy using a range of metrics, such as BLEU and ROUGE, can help to identify errors and inconsistencies in translation performance.*

7.4 Maintenance and Monitoring

The deployment of an AI language model is just the beginning of its lifecycle. To ensure its ongoing effectiveness, it is essential to maintain and monitor its performance over time. This can involve tasks such as model retraining and fine-tuning, as well as monitoring performance metrics such as accuracy and response time. In addition, it is important to monitor for changes in the data distribution or the environment in which the model is deployed, which may require updates or modifications to the model.

For example, consider the deployment of a chatbot for a financial services company. Over time, changes in the types of customer inquiries or the regulations governing the industry may require updates to the chatbot's responses or its underlying model architecture.

7.5 Future Uses

As AI language models continue to evolve, their potential applications are expanding rapidly. From healthcare to customer service, these models have the potential to transform the way we interact with technology. One potential use case is the development of AI-powered virtual assistants that can perform a range of tasks, such as scheduling appointments, answering emails, and providing personalized recommendations. In healthcare, AI language models can be used to analyze medical records, assist with diagnosis, and even predict future health risks.

In the legal industry, AI language models can be used to review legal documents and contracts, saving time and improving accuracy. In customer service, chatbots and virtual assistants can provide 24/7 support.

To further improve the performance of AI language models, it's crucial to follow best practices for their use. Here are some of the best practices to keep in mind:

Use high-quality data: The quality of the data used to train the model is crucial. Make sure the data is relevant and accurate to avoid training a flawed model. Also, ensure that the data is diverse enough to capture different scenarios and contexts.

Fine-tune pre-trained models: Instead of starting from scratch, fine-tuning pre-trained models can save a lot of time and resources. Fine-tuning involves training the model on specific data to adapt it to a specific task. This approach can lead to better performance and faster results.

Evaluate the model: It's essential to evaluate the performance of the model periodically to assess its effectiveness. Use different evaluation metrics to determine how well the model performs on various tasks.

Regularly update the model: Language evolves over time, so the model needs to be updated regularly to reflect changes in language usage. This update can include new words, phrases, and sentence structures that have become popular.

Ensure the model is ethical and unbiased: AI models are only as good as the data they're trained on. If the data is biased, the model will also be biased. Ensure that the data is diverse and unbiased to avoid perpetuating any existing biases. Future uses of AI language models are vast and exciting. One area where AI language models are already making significant progress is in the field of natural language generation (NLG). NLG involves using AI to automatically generate human-like text, such as news articles, product descriptions, and even entire books. AI language models can also be used to improve customer service by providing chatbots that can respond to customer queries effectively. They can also be used to create virtual assistants that can help with tasks such as scheduling appointments, setting reminders, and answering emails.

In conclusion, AI language models are powerful tools that can help individuals and organizations communicate more effectively. By following best practices for their use and exploring their vast potential applications, we can unlock their full potential to improve our lives and drive innovation.

Chapter 07 Back to the Future
The Future of AI Language Models

As I peered into the crystal ball of the future, I couldn't help but wonder what marvels lay ahead for AI language models. It's clear that these intelligent algorithms will continue to play a vital role in our lives and revolutionize the way we communicate.

In the years to come, AI language models will continue to evolve and become even more sophisticated. They'll be able to understand the nuances of human language and provide even more accurate and personalized responses. Imagine having a virtual assistant that not only understands your every need but can also anticipate them before you even ask. But the future of AI language models isn't just about convenience and efficiency. These powerful tools will also play a critical role in advancing research and improving decision-making processes. They can help scientist's process vast amounts of data to make groundbreaking discoveries and help policymakers make informed decisions.

In the world of entertainment, AI language models will also become an integral part of storytelling. Imagine a world where AI can write entire books, creating immersive and captivating worlds that rival even the most creative human minds. Who knows, maybe one day, an AI language model will pen the next best-selling novel, captivating readers with its ability to craft an engaging and compelling story.

But with great power comes great responsibility. As we continue to rely on AI language models, we must also ensure that they're used ethically and without bias. It's crucial to take steps to prevent these powerful tools from perpetuating existing inequalities and biases. In conclusion, the future of AI language models is exciting and full of promise. As we continue to explore their vast potential, we must also take care to use them responsibly and with the utmost care. The possibilities are endless, and I, for one, cannot wait to see what the future holds.

Chapter 08
Case Studies

As I delved into the case studies of AI language model applications, I couldn't help but be amazed by the diverse range of industries that have already begun to harness the power of these intelligent algorithms.

One case study that particularly stood out was in the field of healthcare. Researchers have been exploring the use of AI language models to improve patient outcomes by analyzing large amounts of medical data to predict potential health issues and recommend preventative measures. Imagine a future where AI-powered tools can assist doctors in making faster, more accurate diagnoses, and developing personalized treatment plans for patients. Another fascinating case study was in the field of finance. AI language models have already been employed to analyze market trends and make informed investment decisions, leading to better returns for investors. As these algorithms continue to advance, they may even be able to predict market fluctuations and mitigate potential risks in real-time, transforming the finance industry as we know it.

In the world of customer service, AI language models are already being used to enhance the customer experience by providing personalized and efficient responses to inquiries. Companies like Amazon and Google have already implemented chatbots powered by AI language models, allowing customers to receive quick and accurate answers to their questions 24/7.

But the potential for AI language models doesn't stop there. From transportation to education, there are countless opportunities for these powerful algorithms to transform industries and make our lives easier and more efficient. As we continue to explore these case studies, it's clear that the possibilities for AI language models are endless. We must continue to push the boundaries and explore new use cases to fully unlock their potential and drive innovation forward.

As I continued my research into case studies for AI language models, I discovered several more fascinating examples of how these technologies are being used to transform industries and improve our lives.

In the transportation industry, AI language models are being used to optimize routes, predict traffic patterns, and improve safety on the roads. Companies like Uber and Lyft are already using AI-powered algorithms to suggest the fastest and most efficient routes for their drivers, while also predicting potential accidents or hazards ahead of time. In the future, we may even see self-driving cars powered by AI language models, revolutionizing the way we travel.

In the field of education, AI language models are being used to personalize learning experiences and provide students with customized lesson plans. With the help of these algorithms, teachers can analyze student data and identify areas where students may be struggling, providing them with targeted support and resources to help them succeed. AI language models are also being used to develop language learning apps and other educational tools that can adapt to each student's unique needs and preferences.

In the entertainment industry, AI language models are being used to create more realistic and engaging experiences for audiences. For example, AI-powered chatbots are being developed to interact with viewers during live events, providing them with personalized commentary and insights. AI language models are also being used to create hyper-realistic virtual assistants and characters in video games, bringing new levels of immersion to the gaming experience.

As we look towards the future, the potential uses for AI language models are truly limitless. We may see these technologies being used to power advanced robots and automation systems in manufacturing, or to analyze complex data sets in fields like science and research. In the healthcare industry, AI language models may be used to develop new treatments and cures for diseases, or to help doctors diagnose and treat patients more quickly and accurately. Overall, the case studies for AI language models are truly awe-inspiring. As we continue to push the boundaries of what is possible with these technologies, we are sure to see even more exciting applications emerge in the years to come.

Chapter 09
Building Your Own AI Language Model

Introduction to building your own AI language model

Understanding the basics of machine learning and deep learning

Choosing the right tools and resources for your project

Collecting and preparing your data

Training your model and fine-tuning the parameters

Evaluating the performance of your model

Deploying your model and integrating it into your application or system

Maintaining and updating your model over time

Advanced techniques for improving your model's accuracy and efficiency

Real-world examples of companies and individuals who have built successful AI language models

In this chapter, we will guide you through the process of building your own AI language model, step by step. We will cover everything from the basics of machine learning and deep learning, to choosing the right tools and resources for your project, to collecting and preparing your data, and ultimately training and deploying your model.

We will also discuss advanced techniques for improving your model's accuracy and efficiency, as well as real-world examples of companies and individuals who have built successful AI language models.

By the end of this chapter, you will have the knowledge and skills necessary to create your own AI language model, opening up endless possibilities for innovation and growth in your business or personal projects.

Are you ready to take your AI skills to the next level and build your own AI language model? In this chapter, we will guide you through the process of building a custom language model from start to finish.

Introduction to building your own AI language model

AI language models have become increasingly popular in recent years, powering everything from chatbots to virtual assistants to predictive text. By building your own language model, you can tailor it to your specific needs and use it to solve a wide range of problems.

Understanding the basics of machine learning and deep learning

Before you can build an AI language model, it's important to understand the basics of machine learning and deep learning. We'll cover the fundamentals of these fields, including supervised and unsupervised learning, neural networks, and backpropagation.

Choosing the right tools and resources for your project

There are a variety of tools and resources available for building language models, including open-source libraries like TensorFlow and PyTorch. We'll discuss the pros and cons of different options and help you choose the best one for your project.

Collecting and preparing your data

To build a language model, you'll need a large amount of data to train it on. We'll cover the best practices for collecting and preparing data, including data cleaning, normalization, and augmentation.

Training your model and fine-tuning the parameters

Once you have your data, it's time to train your model. We'll walk you through the process of training a language model, including how to fine-tune the parameters to optimize its performance.

Evaluating the performance of your model

It's important to evaluate the performance of your language model to ensure it's working as intended. We'll discuss common evaluation metrics and techniques, including perplexity and BLEU score.

Deploying your model and integrating it into your application or system

Once your language model is trained and evaluated, it's time to deploy it and integrate it into your application or system. We'll cover the best practices for deployment, including how to handle inputs and outputs and how to scale your model as needed.

Maintaining and updating your model over time

Building an AI language model is just the beginning. It's important to maintain and update your model over time to ensure it stays accurate and up-to-date. We'll discuss best practices for maintenance and updating, including how to handle new data and how to retrain your model as needed.

Advanced techniques for improving your model's accuracy and efficiency

There are a variety of advanced techniques you can use to improve the accuracy and efficiency of your language model, including attention mechanisms, beam search, and transformer architectures. We'll cover these techniques and how to implement them in your own model.

Real-world examples of companies and individuals who have built successful AI language models

Finally, we'll showcase real-world examples of companies and individuals who have built successful AI language models, including chatbots, machine translation systems, and more. By learning from these examples, you'll gain inspiration and ideas for your own language model.

By the end of this chapter, you'll have a solid understanding of the process of building an AI language model and the knowledge and skills to start building your own. With a custom language model, you can take your AI skills to the next level and unlock new possibilities for your business or personal projects.

Before we dive into the technical details, let's first understand what an AI language model is and why building your own model can be beneficial.

An AI language model is a type of machine learning algorithm that is trained on a large corpus of text data to understand the patterns and relationships between words, phrases, and sentences. It can be used for a wide range of natural language processing tasks, such as text classification, sentiment analysis, and language translation.

Building your own AI language model can be beneficial in several ways. First, it allows you to customize the model to your specific needs, which can result in better performance on your specific tasks. Second, it can be more cost-effective than using pre-built models, especially if you have a large amount of data to train your model. Finally, building your own model can give you a better understanding of how AI language models work, which can be helpful in other machine learning and data science projects.

So, how do you build your own AI language model? Here are the basic steps:

Collect and preprocess your data: The first step in building an AI language model is to collect a large corpus of text data and preprocess it to remove any irrelevant information, such as HTML tags or special characters. You may also want to perform additional preprocessing steps such as tokenization and stemming to further clean and standardize the data.

Train the model: Once you have preprocessed your data, you can begin training your model using a machine learning algorithm such as a neural network. There are several open-source libraries and frameworks available for training AI language models, such as TensorFlow, PyTorch, and Hugging Face.

Fine-tune the model: After training the initial model, you may want to fine-tune it on a smaller, more specific dataset to improve its performance on a particular task.

Evaluate the model: Once your model is trained, you should evaluate its performance on a separate test dataset to ensure that it is accurate and robust.

Deploy the model: Finally, you can deploy your AI language model in a variety of ways, depending on your needs. For example, you can integrate it into a web application, use it to generate text for a chatbot, or incorporate it into a larger machine learning pipeline.

Building your own AI language model can be a challenging and time-consuming process, but it can also be incredibly rewarding. With the right data and tools, you can create a powerful language model that can help you solve a wide range of natural language processing tasks.

Building your own AI language model can be a challenging but rewarding task. With the right tools and knowledge, you can create a model that is customized to your specific needs and requirements. Whether you're looking to improve customer service, automate certain tasks, or simply experiment with the latest advancements in AI, building your own language model can open up a whole new world of possibilities. As with any new technology, it's important to stay up-to-date with the latest developments and best practices, but with the right approach, your AI language model can become your new secret weapon for success.

AI Language Models: Your New Secret Weapon is a comprehensive guide to understanding and utilizing AI language models to enhance communication and productivity. This book covers the basics of natural language processing, advanced techniques for improving language models, use cases for AI language models, and best practices for implementation. It also includes case studies of successful implementation and a step-by-step guide for building your own language model.

The future of AI language models is also explored, with insights into the latest advancements and potential applications in various industries. Written in an engaging and accessible style, this book is perfect for anyone looking to stay ahead of the curve and leverage the power of AI language models in their business or personal projects. Whether you're a beginner or an experienced developer, AI Language Models: Your New Secret Weapon is an essential resource for anyone interested in the world of AI language models.